First published in the United States and Canada in 2022 by B.E.S. Publishing.

Text © 2022 by Pat Thomas
Illustrations © 2022 by Hodder and Stoughton
Illustrations by Leslie Harker

Cover and internal design © 2022 by Sourcebooks

Published by Sourcebooks eXplore an imprint of Sourcebooks Kids
P.O. Box 4410, Naperville, Illinois 60567–4410
(630) 961–3900
sourcebookskids.com

Cataloging-in-Publication Data is on file with the Library of Congress.

Source of Production: RR Donnelley Asia Printing Solutions Ltd., Dongguan, Guangdong Province, China
Date of Production: 04/2022

Printed and bound in China.
RRD 10 9 8 7 6 5 4 3 2 1

MY BUSY BRAIN

A FIRST LOOK AT ADHD

Written by
PAT THOMAS

Illustrated by
LESLIE HARKER

sourcebooks
eXplore

Do you know what it's like to feel full of energy and excited? To want to talk and laugh and run around, rather than sit still or take your turn or listen quietly?

We all feel like
that sometimes.

But some people feel like that all the time.

They can get excited or frustrated or angry really quickly, and then find it hard to calm down again.

They may have difficulty listening to others and can get distracted or bored really easily.

Being this way can make them forgetful and disorganised. It can make it hard to finish things like chores and homework.

When you feel like this all the time, it could be because you have what is called Attention Deficit Hyperactivity Disorder, or ADHD.

That's a lot of big words, and it may sound scary. But all it means is that your brain works differently from other people's brains.

WHAT ABOUT YOU?

Do you have ADHD or do you know someone who does? Can you think of some ways that person thinks and acts differently from others?

With ADHD, your brain feels busy all the time. It can make it hard to figure out the difference between big and little problems.

It can make it difficult to sit still or concentrate on learning things like reading, spelling and maths.

It can make it hard to control your thoughts and feelings and to understand how the things you do affect others...

...and that can make it hard to make friends.

Nobody is sure what causes ADHD. It could come from our genes, which are the instruction manuals for how our bodies and minds work and what we look like.

All families share some genes, which is why they can look and act alike and even have some of the same health conditions.

Having ADHD isn't easy. It can make you feel like you are different from everyone else and that you don't fit in.

Sometimes other people can be mean about it. They may make fun of you or try to tell you that you are "lazy" or "slow" or "selfish" or "rude."

None of those things are true.

We are all a little bit different and we all have things
that we are good at—and things that we are not so good at.

No one does everything well,
and everyone needs help sometimes.

When you have ADHD, you may have a therapist or counselor who you can talk to and who helps you understand your feelings. Some people with ADHD may take medicine to help them.

WHAT ABOUT YOU?

What are some of the things you are good at?
What are some of the things you are not so good at?

Your family
and teachers
and friends
can help, too.
They can remind
you to take breaks,
to calm down,
and to finish
what you start.

They can help
you take care
of your body
and brain by
eating good food,
getting enough
sleep, and getting
lots of exercise.

ADHD is not the same in every person
and everyone who has it needs to find the
different kinds of help that work best for them.

Anyone can have
ADHD—even grown-ups—and some
people who have it also have special talents
and abilities. They can be creative and energetic.
They can be funny and ask lots of interesting questions.

But even though ADHD can have a positive side, it's never an excuse for shouting or hurting other people or breaking the rules.

There's no right way
or wrong way to feel about
having ADHD.

Some days it will feel great...

...and other days it will feel terrible and confusing.

Whatever you feel about it is OK.

ADHD is a part of who you are, but it's not all of who you are.

You might not outgrow it, but you can learn to control it and focus all that extra energy on the things you are really good at.

Lots of famous and successful people
who have ADHD—including athletes,
actors, musicians and politicians
—have learned to do this.

If they can do it,
you can do it, too.

HOW TO USE THIS BOOK

This book provides a simple introduction to Attention Deficit Hyperactivity Disorder (ADHD). Its aim is to promote understanding and ongoing discussion with children who have ADHD or those who have siblings or classmates with it. It explains, in child-friendly terms, what ADHD is and what it feels like from the child's perspective. It also acknowledges the difficulties that those who do not have ADHD sometimes have in understanding those who do.

Try reading it the book first and familiarising yourself with its content before you begin. The "What about you?" questions throughout the text can be useful prompts for understanding things from your child's point of view. You may find benefit in reading the book with your child more than once. Repetition allows young children to formulate thoughts and questions as the need arises. When you are ready to talk to a child about ADHD consider the following points:

Call it what it is. A diagnosis of ADHD can feel like a heavy burden for a child to bear. It's understandable that parents might want to resist that "label" and reassure children they are not sick or even resist strategies that single their child out as "different". But consider that it may be worse for your child to be labeled disruptive, lazy or slow—as can so often happen. Calling ADHD what it is gives you options for coping and for helping your child avoid other painful or negative labels.

Focus on the positive. Help your child understand they are more than their diagnosis. Children with ADHD can have low self-esteem, so make the effort to reinforce the positive aspects of who they are, and praise their talents and skills so that they understand that even with ADHD they can pursue their interests and achieve. Help them to understand that no one is good at everything. We all have things we have to try harder to be good at.

Make time to listen. It is easy for adult interaction with ADHD children to become all about organisation, supervision and management and trying to help them "fit in." Always trying to fit in or adapt can be exhausting for everyone so remember to take time to listen to what your child says about their feelings and needs. Listening and acceptance are as important as nudging their behavior in a direction that helps them thrive at home, school and in social settings.

Don't make promises you can't keep. It's tempting to tell your child that they will "grow out of it." This doesn't always happen, although as children get older it can become easier to manage ADHD. Having ADHD is not a straight path and there may be phases where your child seems to get worse before they start to improve again. Instead of promising your child they will get "better," reassure them that you will always be there to support and love them.

Dealing with emotional outbursts. Defiance and emotional outbursts can be common with ADHD. Children may have a low tolerance for frustration anyway, but outbursts can also be a normal emotional reaction to always being asked to do things that are difficult or not enjoyable. This is why daily routines like doing homework, getting dressed, taking turns and going to bed can quickly become battlegrounds. Help your child by staying calm yourself and by providing as much stability and consistency in their routine as possible. If constant verbal reminders are a trigger, try making a poster of all the things your child needs to do each day.

If your child needs medication. ADHD is primarily a brain chemistry disorder. For some children it may be severe enough to require medication. Many parents take great care not to frame ADHD as a sickness and this can lead to some tricky discussions about medication use. It's tempting to refer to ADHD medicine as similar to vitamins, but this is misleading and can even lead children to believe that more is better, which is not the case with drugs. Try instead to frame medication in the same way as needing glasses to see better or needing to avoid certain foods you are allergic to.

How teachers can help. Parents, teachers and therapists all have a key role to play in helping children with ADHD. Kids get better at paying attention, slowing down and gaining self-control. Working with parents they can help teach children with ADHD do well in class with actions such as breaking schoolwork into parts, helping ADHD kids stay organised, seating kids in places where they won't get distracted (such as away from a window or door), and where possible giving kids with ADHD small breaks to get up and move during class. Children with ADHD often don't have the language to explain it to others, so teachers also have a vital role to play in helping classmates understand, rather than stigmatise, ADHD.

FURTHER READING

Squirmy Wormy: How I Learned to Help Myself
Lynda Farrington Wilson (Future Horizons, 2020)

The Trouble with Dragons
Conrad Robson and Ben Kaberry (ADHD Foundation, 2018)
Downloadable from the ADHD Foundation UK website

When My Worries Get Too Big! A Relaxation Book for Children Who Live With Anxiety
Kari Dunn Buron (AAPC Publishing, 2013)

All Dogs Have ADHD
Kathy Hoopmann (Jessica Kingsley Publishers, 2020)

A Walk in the Rain With a Brain
Edward Hallowell, MD (Harper Collins, 2004)

USEFUL WEBSITES

ADHD Foundation UK
www.adhdfoundation.org.uk

Attention Deficit Disorder Association
www.add.org

CHADD (Children and Adults with Attention-Deficit/Hyperactivity Disorder)
www.chadd.org

Child Mind Institute
www.childmind.org

ADDitude
www.additudemag.com